Sugar
Spice

& lessons for life

May God's Richest & Best Be yours

[signature] 6/12/08

Sugar Spice

& lessons for life

A father's words of faith for his daughter

Steven Hood

TATE PUBLISHING *& Enterprises*

Sugar, Spice, and Lessons for Life
Copyright © 2008 by Steven Hood. All rights reserved.

This title is also available as a Tate Out Loud product. Visit www.tatepublishing.com for more information.

No part of this publication may be reproduced, stored in a retrieval system or transmitted in any way by any means, electronic, mechanical, photocopy, recording or otherwise without the prior permission of the author except as provided by USA copyright law.

Scripture quotations marked "NIV" are taken from the *Holy Bible, New International Version* ®, Copyright © 1973, 1978, 1984 by International Bible Society. Used by permission of Zondervan Publishing House. All rights reserved.

Scripture quotations marked "NLT" are taken from the Holy Bible, New Living Translation, Copyright © 1996. Used by permission of Tyndale House Publishers, Inc. All rights reserved.

The opinions expressed by the author are not necessarily those of Tate Publishing, LLC.

Published by Tate Publishing & Enterprises, LLC
127 E. Trade Center Terrace | Mustang, Oklahoma 73064 USA
1.888.361.9473 | www.tatepublishing.com

Tate Publishing is committed to excellence in the publishing industry. The company reflects the philosophy established by the founders, based on Psalm 68:11,
"The Lord gave the word and great was the company of those who published it."

Book design copyright © 2008 by Tate Publishing, LLC. All rights reserved.
Cover design by Leah LeFlore
Interior design by Joey Garrett

Published in the United States of America

ISBN: 978-1-60462-980-4
1. Christian Living: Practical Life
2. Christian Living: General Interest
08.05.16

To My Daughter Kendra,
I did not give you my blood or my genes;
I gave you my heart.
I love you,
Dad

Table of Contents

A father's words of faith for his daughter.

11   Recipes for Life

17   Recipes for Grace

25   Recipes for Love

35   Recipes for Wisdom

49   Recipes for Success

59   Recipes for the Proverbs 31 Woman

69   Recipes for Happiness

Introduction

Over the ages, parents have passed down to their children lessons, recipes if you will, to live by. As you grew up, I gave you as many recipes as I could at the time. They were mostly short-term recipes, given as an immediate lesson, a bandage for a wound, instructions for the day or for the evening, or discipline for a botched attempt to do it by yourself.

The revision of this book is designed to give you more than just recipes for the kitchen, although there are more that have been added. The additional pages are now included to give you true recipes for life. In just two short years you have gone from a single woman, only caring for yourself and your own needs, to a wife and mother. You now have a husband to care for and support. As well, you also have a son and a daughter to raise. Your responsibilities now revolve around your family and your home.

There were many recipes that I had not passed along until now. You were not ready for them. As with any good recipe, it requires a certain amount of discipline to make the dish correctly: following directions, combining the right ingredients at the right time in the right amount, knowing how much heat to use, knowing when to apply pressure, when to cool off, and when to freeze; these are all a part of the discipline of cooking and of life. As I have watched you over the past two years, you have grown and matured into the woman that you are today. It is time now to pass along these recipes—your recipes for life.

> God,
> I ask that you add your blessings of life on these recipes. I ask that you direct my words and my recipes to my daughter. Season them with your Holy Spirit. Let your grace and love be seen in each dish prepared. And when the time is right, let these same recipes be passed on to each generation to follow.
> In the name of Jesus Christ, our Lord,
>
> So let it be.

Recipes for Life

> Today I have given you the choice between life and death, between blessings and curses. I call on heaven and earth to witness the choice you make. Oh, that you would choose life, that you and your descendants might live.
>
> Duet 30:19 (NLT)

There are many choices that we make through life. Some are inconsequential; what to eat, what to wear, etc., while some choices have such far-reaching effects that the consequences of these choices are seen by our children and grand-children. Who do I marry? Where will we live? What will I do for work, for a career? These were the major choices that were made by my parents. In today's world the choices are even more profound. Drugs, pornography, sex outside of marriage, STDs,

AIDS, false religion versus true faith, and the list goes on. These are choices that are not only life changing, but life altering, and in some cases life ending.

In the book of Deuteronomy, Moses spells out the law of God to the nation of Israel on the last days before they cross the Jordan River into the Promised Land. These laws, recipes if you will, were about life. These recipes that God gave to Moses, if they were followed, gave life to the people. Much like food and drink gives life to us, God's word also gives life to us, and those words of life were the ingredients that God gave through Moses, to His people.

After God gave these words (ingredients) of life to the nation of Israel, He gave them a choice: they could choose to use these ingredients for a good and whole life, or they could reject them and try to make it up on their own. What a wonderful and extraordinary thing it is that the God of the entire universe would give us His creation and the right and ability to choose. Do we choose to use the ingredients that God has given us? Or do we choose to make it up ourselves? God allows us to decide.

Along with giving the nation of Israel a choice, God showed them the consequences of that choice, both good and bad. If they chose to follow God and the recipe for life that He laid out for them, there was a long list of blessings—special gifts from God—that they would receive. They would be blessed wherever they lived, whether in the city or in the country. They would be blessed with having a large and loving family. Their work would be blessed in the crops, cattle, and sheep that they raised, and they would prosper in all that they would do. They would be blessed by God's protection from their enemies. And all of these blessings would be passed on to their children and grand-children and great grand-children, as long as they continued to follow the Lord their God.

However, if they did not choose to follow God and tried to make up their own recipes for living, the consequences were as bad as the blessings were good. Pretty much all that they tried to do outside of God's will would be cursed and their lives would come to ruin. All of this is found in the 28th chapter of Deuteronomy, and all of this applies to us today; both the blessings for following God, and the curses for living our lives apart from God.

In cooking, sometimes you can get lucky and find the right combinations of flavors and spices and create something out of nothing on your own. My most famous creation along these lines is the "Mexican Dish" that was born out of too much month at the end of our money. More often than not, our efforts to create came out just a little bit off. It was not quite what we intended, or in some cases, absolutely not edible. We need a recipe; a set of instructions to follow created by someone with years of experience and practical knowledge. God gave us such a recipe. It is called the Bible.

The Bible is God's gift to us and contains all the recipes for our life. It gives us all the ingredients that we will need and how to use these ingredients to create a happy and healthy life. It is in our choosing these ingredients that we gain life and blessings for ourselves, and not only for ourselves, but also for our children as we feed them from these recipes.

As with any recipe, you first have to sit down and read it all the way through to understand it. You have to know what ingredients you are going to need, what instruments you will need to use, if it will be cooked in the oven or on the stove, or if it will be frozen after it is finished. The same is true for God's recipe for life. You need to read it through to get a clear picture of the dish that God has made available for you. The good news is that you do not need to provide all of the ingredients and will not have to bring any cooking utensils. God has provided it all, and the only thing that you will need to bring is your heart.

If you haven't started reading the Bible, today is a good day to start. You might try reading one chapter a day at first. Keep to it, and in no time at all you will have gone all the way through. I always start at the first book of the New Testament, Matthew. After reading through the New Testament, then go after the Old Testament.

You will be amazed at how quickly it goes, and how much you will enjoy that time each day.

With that in mind, let us go on to look at these recipes for life that God gives us. Put your apron on and get the oven heated up. God has many wonderful recipes to teach us. Let's go look at a few!

Bon appetite!

Recipes for Grace

For it is by Grace that you have been saved, through faith—and this not from yourselves, it is the gift of God—not of works, so that no one can boast.

Eph 2:8–9 (NIV)

God saved you by His special favor when you believed. And you can't take any credit for this; it is a gift from God. Salvation is not a reward for the good things we have done, so none of us can boast about it.

Eph 2:8–9 (NLT)

What is grace, and why is it so important to understand this concept, this special recipe in our lives? We understand that grace is the ability to move about without falling down or bumping into things as we are growing up. And we are occasionally called "Grace" when we make an obviously ungraceful move. But what does this word actually mean, what is this recipe all about?

A good definition of grace comes to mind from a lesson that I learned long ago. I remember sitting in an adult Sunday school class one morning. I was with a friend who was a guest teacher that day. I forget what the lesson was about, but I do remember the conversation got around to the word *saved*. A woman spoke up and said that she had a problem with the word *saved* and believed that a better word should be used there. Being a guest at the time, I kept quiet, but I remember thinking that if she had a problem with that word *saved*, she probably was not.

Being saved simply means that you are completely without hope of helping yourself out of the situation that you are in. Everything you have tried did not work, and without help, you are going to die. Someone is going to have to intervene, someone is going to have to step up and rescue you.

Consider it this way. You have just fallen out of a boat in the middle of the Pacific Ocean. You have no life raft, no life vest, you don't know how to swim, and you have no hope of ever seeing another boat. There are sharks just below the surface, biding their time until they are ready to devour you. All you can see around you is mile upon mile of ocean. If you could swim, you wouldn't even know which way to go! Alone and adrift, as small as a grain of sand in the middle of a desert, absolutely hopeless, about to be eaten alive; this is the condition of your life.

Suddenly, out of nowhere, a boat appears and a hand reaches out and snatches you out of this watery grave. You were not expecting it, you did nothing to cause this boat to show up, you paid nothing to this person to rescue you, and you had done nothing in your life to deserve this rescue. He simply saw you drowning, soon to be eaten by the sharks, and because of His love for you, reached out His hand and pulled you out.

Now here is the amazing part, you had a choice at that time to accept His offer of rescue or continue to try on you own to save yourself. This seems absolutely amazing that anybody in that position would refuse His help but many do. God's amazing grace is still a choice for all of us. It is truly the choice between life and death.

All of us are drifting in a sea called *sin*, and there is no way that we can escape from it by ourselves. We can't be good enough, or do enough good deeds, or just try to act right or be nicer to people. There are not enough good works in this world to save us, because it is that one bad thing, that one sin that cancels out all the good works we do.

Consider, if you will, the recipe for an omelet. You take a few eggs, some milk, some ham or bacon, some cheese, and whatever else you like, mix all of this in a bowl and cook it in a skillet. Now, consider that you have combined all of these ingredients and are getting ready to crack the last egg into the mixture. As it falls into the bowl, it becomes clearly evident that this egg was rotten. Now it is too late. The omelet is ruined. You can't get it back out because it has touched and contaminated all of the good parts that you have already put in. All of your good work to that point has now been ruined.

Sin does the same thing in our lives. In God's eye, sin is sin no matter how small or large. Without God's saving grace, you will go to hell for telling a lie or for committing rape or murder, there is no difference. Therefore we need a Savior that requires nothing of us except our acceptance of His free gift of salvation. That is what God provides for us in His son, Jesus Christ. Through His death on the cross, He took on his body all of our sins, mine and yours, and killed them with Him as He died. And through His resurrection to life, He gives us the opportunity to live with Him forever. It is our choice to accept this free gift, this outstretched hand to pull us out of the ocean of sin that we are dying in. Have you accepted this gift?

I would be amiss if I did not ask that last question. It is the most important question that you will ever answer. God is not going to ask where you lived or what kind of car you drove or how you dressed. God is not going to ask if you went to church or stayed home (although we should be involved in His work). God is going to ask you why He should let you into heaven. Did you accept His free gift of grace or reject it? That is going to be His final question and your answer will determine where you will spend eternity.

Maybe you want to pray this prayer right now to settle this issue once and for all: God, I am a sinner and I am hopelessly lost in this world. I have tried and failed many times to save myself by being good enough and doing good things for people, but I have always failed in the end. Forgive me and save me. I accept your free gift of grace and salvation for my life, and I will live my life for you from here forward. I thank you, Jesus, for loving me and saving me. So be it!

So, what do we do with this recipe for grace? We make it a part of every meal that we make in our lives. All of our life and all that we do should be seasoned with a large measure of grace. Grace for ourselves and grace for others; this has to be the first and key ingredient in all of our recipes. Since God has poured such a large measure of grace on us, we must in turn pour that same grace out to all those around us. The people that we encounter in our day to day life, people that we work with, our neighbors, the person standing in line with you at the store, the guy that pulled out in front of you or cut you off on the street (now I've gone to meddling), all of these people need to see God's grace in you. And, you need to pass that grace along to them in their time of need.

We must give out an extra measure of grace to our family. These are the people who often are the last on our list, yet are the closest to us, and sometimes are the people who most need a touch of God's grace in their lives. How many times do we hear the story of a death or divorce or illness, and we say, "Gosh, I never knew anything was wrong!" Your words to your family members may have more impact than you will ever know. A kind word at just the right time, an encouraging word, a word to motivate, a word to heal, you just never know how God will use your words. Therefore, season your words heavily with God's grace and you will never go wrong.

Let every recipe in your life reflect the measure of grace that God has poured out on you. There is a story that is told about a time when Jesus went in to eat supper at the house of one of the religious leaders of His time. There were a number of guests for dinner that night, all of them from the local church, and they had gathered to hear what Jesus was teaching. Among the crowd there was a woman who came in from the streets. She had made her way in through the crowd and simply wanted to worship the person that she knew was her Savior.

The people from the church saw this woman come in, and they were appalled as they watched her fall at the feet of Jesus, washing His feet with her tears and wiping them dry with her hair. They were also amazed as she poured an entire bottle of costly perfume on His feet. They talked among themselves, wondering why He would let such a woman touch Him. If He were a prophet, the true Son of God, He should know what type of woman this was.

Jesus, knowing their hearts and knowing the heart of the woman at His feet, told them this: "I tell you, her sins—and they are many—have been forgiven, so she has shown me much love. But a person who is forgiven little shows only a little love" (Luke 7:47, NLT). Jesus then sent her on her way in peace, forgiven and healed. The rest of the crowd stood around discussing if the word *saved* was the appropriate word to use.

As grace abounds in your life, season the lives of all those around you. This is not an ingredient to be used sparingly, with just a pinch here or a dash there. Pour out grace in large quantities over every recipe of your life. This gift of grace was given to you for free; therefore, freely and generously give it out.

Recipes for Love

> Submit to one another out of reverence for Christ. Wives, submit to your husbands as to the Lord. Husbands, love your wives, just as Christ loved the church and gave himself up for her, each one of you also must love his wife as he loves himself, and the wife must respect her husband.
>
> Eph 5: 21, 22, 25, 33 (NIV)

So much has been said over the years about love, that it is hard to know where to start. Do we prepare this dish from the physical or emotional level? Do we get into the deep, intellectual discussions about the ingredients for love and how to blend them? Maybe we chop it up into small bits that can be mixed in with all of the other recipes for life?

I believe that the scripture mentioned above gives us the base or the starting ingredients for our recipe for love.

Love, in its purest sense, begins and ends in the home, and it gets its start with marriage. God gave marriage to us, and also, He gave us a very real way to make it work. This all revolves around a very small but extremely volatile word—*submit*. This word has been the source of everything from round-table discussions to all-out war. And yet it is the word that God chose to use to teach us about love.

So what is the definition of the word *submit*? Webster's dictionary gives us the following: "To yield to governance or authority, to yield oneself to the authority or will of another: surrender b: to permit oneself to be subjected to something, to defer to or consent to abide by the opinion or authority of another."

Submit is the ingredient of this recipe for love that is most often left out. As we create our love dish, we add healthy portions of sex, generous sprinkles of fun and laughter, several scoops of understanding and appreciation, and a dusting of talk time at the end of the day. So where does *submit* fit into the recipe for love? It fits in at the start, it is blended into the middle, and it is added again at the very end.

The first thing that we are told to do in our relationships is to submit to one another. That means submission is not a one way street, as some would want you to believe. It is to be practiced by both husband and wife in an act of love. Any ingredient in our recipe for love must be added in equal parts by both the husband and the wife. If one adds more than the other, it will take on the flavor of that individual and not of the two. When submission is a one-way street, the flavor is often very bitter and usually results in a ruined dish. However, when added in equal parts, the flavors compliment each other, allowing a full range of spices to continue to be added.

When we use the word *submit*, what is meant? Submitting is not becoming a doormat for your husband. Submitting is not being his slave or waitress. Submitting is not cowering in the corner, waiting for your next order from the master. Submitting is the understanding of your role and your husbands role in the home and in your marriage. As each business has an organizational structure, so does a marriage. You are both given duties in you marriage, and as a wife and mother, you have a certain job description.

Sometimes these duties will overlap, such as you taking out the trash or your husband washing the dishes, but on the main duties, your marriage and your life will always work better if you keep to the roles that you were given. Be supportive but don't withhold your opinion. Be respectful and ask for that same respect to be given back. Be loving and caring to one another, because both of you work in a world that is not. Submit to your husband's authority, just as he has submitted to Gods authority in his life. These are the "equal parts" mentioned above. Each of you, submitting to the authority of God in your life and in your lives together, this is what the scripture teaches, and this is the first ingredient in our recipe for love.

The second key ingredient in our recipe for love is selflessness. This is a mighty big word that just simply means to care more about others (your spouse) than yourself. To be selfless is to be available to your husband at the end of his long day, when your day has been just as long. To be selfless is to give a foot massage or back massage even when you don't feel like it. To be selfless is to give to others, whether it is of your time or money or both, when you are the one in need. To be selfless is to love more than you know how and to give more than you have to give.

Jesus gives us the definition of selflessness in the life that He lived on this earth. The one who was God in human flesh came to this earth not to be served but to serve others and ultimately to give His life as a sacrifice for the sin in our lives. His life gave us a picture of how we should live ours. To serve others not looking for gratitude or reward, to give love even when it is not returned, to lend without any thought of being repaid, to lay down our life so others might live; this is selflessness. This ingredient is always to be added in equal parts by both the husband and the wife. Mutually giving oneself to each other creates the trust and love that will season your relationship for a lifetime.

There are a number of other ingredients for our recipe for love that starts at home. They are found in the 13th chapter of Paul's first letter to the church in Corinth and are as follows: patience, kindness, trusting (not jealous), humility (not boastful or proud), giving (not demanding its own way), happiness (not irritable), forgiving, and forgetful (keeps no record of wrongs), expectation of right justice, persistence, faithfulness, hopefulness, and endurance. Blend all of these ingredients in generous quantities. As your love grows over the years, the amounts of these ingredients will vary. Some years you will need to add an extra measure of patience, in some seasons you will need a double dose of forgiveness. Each change of the year and the seasons of life will bring about the need to add a little more of one spice over the other.

The final and most important ingredient to add in our recipe for love that starts at home is the love from God. The love of God will seal your love for each other against all the ravages of this world. The truth is, we can stand alone and fight, winning only a few. We can stand together as a couple and fight and win a handful more. Or we can stand as a couple, bound together by the love of God and win them all. May God strengthen your love for each other with the love that He has for you both.

Having finished this recipe for love in the home, let's

also look at a recipe for love that goes beyond the front door. Love for our family, our friends, our neighbors, and yes, even our in-laws are included in this next recipe. It is really a very simple recipe, and yet is used and shared less and less each year. So, let's take a look!

There is a story in the Bible that tells about a conversation between Jesus and a religious leader of that day. The question was asked which commandment from God was the greatest. Jesus responded by saying that we should love the Lord our God with all of our heart, with all of our mind, and with all of our strength. Then Jesus added that we should love our neighbors as much as we love ourselves. This, He said, was the sum of all the words of the prophets and all of the Jewish law.

The first ingredient in our recipe for love outside the home is an unending portion of love for God and devotion to Him. It is only when we find ourselves truly in love with God above all others and beyond all else that we are able to love ourselves and everybody else. How is this so? If we are so dedicated and devoted to God, how can we think of or love anybody else? Ah, this is what makes this ingredient so special. The more we focus on God and our devotion to Him, the more God will focus us on others around us. The small measure of love that we give to God is mixed in with His unending amount of love and is poured back into our lives. So much so that we have to go out and share it with everyone that we meet.

It is like the story of the rock soup. It seems that one evening a group of boys were sitting around the campfire after a long day of work on the ranch. There was a pot of water boiling on the fire and in the pot was a rock. Now all the boys were hungry and each had been given a certain ration of food for the day, but it wasn't very much. The boy making the rock soup said to the others that it was just about finished and he gave it a taste. "Hmm," said the boy. "This tastes real good but it could use a little more flavor. Do any of you have a potato that you would like to add?" A boy came forward and said that the rancher had given him a sack of potatoes as his ration of food, and he would gladly peel some up for the soup. After cooking these for a little while, it was tasted again. "This is getting pretty good now, but does anybody have a carrot they would like to add?" Another boy jumped up and said that the rancher had given him a sack of carrots, and he would gladly add some. As the evening went on and the periodic tasting of the rock soup continued, each boy would volunteer a part of the rations that the rancher had given to them. After the potatoes and carrots came some onions, peppers, tomatoes, beef jerky, and on and on until finally they had a soup fit for a king and plenty of it to go around.

Our love for God is much like the rock soup. All by itself, it is going to be bland and flavorless, lacking any nutritional value and small in its portion. But, as God begins to add His ingredients to it, the soup becomes a truly nutritious meal. As well, as God adds more ingredients to it, the pot will become fuller and fuller, making a meal not just for you, but for all of the hungry people around. Therefore as we open our hearts to God, He will open His heart to us so much so that we must go out and share it. Sharing God's love is our next ingredient!

The love that God gives us was never meant to be held on to. This love was meant to be shared with our family, our friends, our neighbors, our co-workers, and pretty much anyone we come into contact with during our day to day lives. The sharing ingredient in this recipe allows us to take God's love with us everywhere we go. As you go about your daily routine, how simple is it to give a smile to a stranger as you walk by. How simple is it to say "Please and Thank you," those magic words that we learned a long time ago. How simple is it to hold the door for someone or to allow them into a line at the check-out or at the stop light. As simple as all of this is, why not do it every day? What a simple, yet effective way to spread the love of God to all you meet.

Too many times we feel that we must be doing missionary work in Africa to be spreading love outside the home. Sometimes the missionary work that we are called to do is right in our own neighborhood or at our place of work or even within our own family.

When Jesus sent out His disciples, he told them to go to the streets of Jerusalem, the cities of Judea, Samaria, and to the farthest parts of the earth. However, the first place he told them to go to minister was in their home town. Often we miss that and believe that we must go to outer Mongolia and live with Tibetan monks to serve God. Often God would have us not go any farther than the end of our street. And if you look hard enough, the mission field of your own backyard will be where God will direct you and where you will see His power at work. Therefore, take every opportunity you have to spread God's love. Whether it is inside your home or out in your neighborhood, it is a wonderful dish to be shared with all.

Recipes for Wisdom

> The fear of the Lord is the beginning of wisdom.
> Only fools despise wisdom and discipline.
>
> Proverbs 1:7 (NLT)

When we consider the recipe and ingredients for wisdom, let's look at the person who is considered the master chef of wisdom: Solomon. The story is told that when Solomon became king of Israel, he had a dream that he was talking with God. God said to the new king, "What do you want? Ask and I will give it to you." Solomon's response was to ask God for an understanding mind (wisdom), that he could govern God's people justly. This greatly pleased God, and with that, Solomon was endowed with wisdom beyond any other human before or since, except for Jesus, since He was God in the flesh. Because of Solomon's answer, God also blessed him with all of the material possessions the world could offer and with a long and healthy life.

Therefore, let's look at the words and wisdom of God through Solomon for the ingredients of this recipe. Our ingredients will include:

- Knows God
- Respects and fears God
- Puts God first
- Trusts in the Lord
- Turns away from evil
- Knows right from wrong
- Chooses to do right
- Self control
- Listens and learns
- Loves correction and discipline
- Responds correctly to correction
- Teachable
- Love for people
- Disdain for pride, arrogance, and evil
- Faithful to your word
- Give good and sound advice

These ingredients are grouped together much like spices are mixed together to create a unique flavor. The first of these is the mixture of God in your life. As with all of these recipes for life, God is the first ingredient, and in this recipe for wisdom, a heavy dose of God is added. All wisdom begins and ends with God, and in our recipe for wisdom, we must first know God.

Knowing God intimately, not just having head knowledge of God is what is required. It is the difference between having a friend and having a best friend. Your best friend knows you better than anybody else. They know all of your good and bad points and are still your friend in spite of them. They know when you're having a bad day and will sit with you to hear all about it. They celebrate all the good times with you and cheer you on to further victories. And sometimes they are just there to sit quietly with you, not saying a word and not needing to say a word. This is knowing God, and that is the first spice that is put into this mix.

The second part of this spice mix is the respect and fear of the Lord. The fear of the Lord is not talked about very much today. And if we are living under God's grace, we don't have to dwell on this a great deal. However, it is important to understand that the God of the entire universe, who created everything with just a word from His mouth, He holds us in the palm of His hand. It is a fearful thing, if you are outside of God's love and grace. True wisdom comes from this understanding.

With this understanding, we put God first in our lives. In all that we do, all that we have, and all that we are, God is first and foremost. Jesus taught us this as he spoke to the people of His day. He told us not to worry about what we would eat or what we would wear or where we would live. He said that God already knows about all of those needs, and if we would put Him first in our lives, then all of these needs (and all of the needs of our lives) would be met.

Next comes the toughest part, the spiciest of the spices, *trust*. God spoke through Solomon and said this, "Trust in the Lord with all of your heart and do not lean on your own understanding. Acknowledge Him in all of your ways and He will make your path straight" (Proverbs 3:5–6, NIV).

When you truly know God as a friend, when you put God first in your life, when you can put yourself into the hands of almighty God in all situations—this gives you the base for a true and pure mix of these spices for wisdom. It is only after we add trust to this mix that it is complete.

God tells us throughout His word to trust Him. Hundreds of stories are told about this trust, of those who did trust Him and their wonderful reward, and of those who did not and the terrible punishment they endured.

One of my favorite stories comes from the book of 2nd Chronicles, in the 20th chapter. Here we find the story of

King Jehoshaphat. It happened on this day (had to be a Monday) that he received a report from the messengers of his army. There were three nations that had declared war on him and his kingdom and were already on their way to wipe them out. Upon hearing this news, the king immediately called for fasting and prayer throughout the whole nation. His first steps were to go to God. Too often when we find ourselves in bad situations we try many other ways to fix it, bandage it, or even hide it before we go to God. The king knew better and did not waste any time looking for another way out.

God honored the king's right decision and honored his trust. God told the king to not be afraid or discouraged by the enormous army that was marching against him. This battle belonged to God, and God would take care of it. The king simply had to trust God, to take Him at His word, and do what he was told: go out to the battlefield, take up his position, then stand still and watch.

As it turned out, God caused these three armies to turn against each other, and not one of them were left standing at the end of the day. The king and his army did not lift one finger in the battle. And after it was over, they went down to carry off the plunder, which took three days because there was so much. This was God's reward for their trust.

I could go on for many more pages, relating more of my favorite stories of trust, but I will let you find your own favorites in the Bible. It means much more when God opens His word to your heart and shows you these same stories. Let's just say this: a wise person is known not by the words of their mouth, but by the actions of their life. Trusting God is not a word from your mouth, it is a way of life; it is an act of your will to believe that God is a good God, and that He will always lead you down the right and straightest path.

The second ingredient to wisdom is really a two part mixture: knowing right from wrong and choosing to do right. This is a mixture that when one part is missing, the other part of it just isn't quite right.

We get to make a lot of choices in our recipe for life. And there are a lot of ingredients that can be used. Some work well, while others are clearly not the right choice. Wisdom has, as its most simple ingredient, the knowledge of what is right and what is wrong and with that, the ability to choose right over wrong.

Let's start at the beginning; Adam and Eve. In the beginning, these two knew God face to face. They spent time walking with God in the garden and talking about all of God's beautiful creation. God gave them some very specific instructions about what to eat and about what not to eat. It was made very clear to them what the right thing to do was, and sure enough, they chose to do the wrong thing. This was not wisdom in action.

Okay, fast forward a few thousand years to Jesus

Christ. Jesus walked with His Father and talked face to face with Him. And we get to know the character of Jesus through just a small sampling of His conversations with God. In one of His best known conversations with God, Jesus was at the point of making a choice. He knew what was right, and He also knew how much pain and suffering He would have to endure to do the right thing. In possibly the wisest act on the face of the earth, Jesus chose to do the right thing. He chose to obey God and die for you and for me. And through His obedience, He was raised back to life, giving us the opportunity to live with Him for eternity.

How many choices do we face each day? Most of the time, we know the right choice to make. Now, we may agonize over the choices and ask others for their opinion, but most of the time, we already know what we should do. The question now becomes: Do we choose to do right? Wisdom is proved by what we chose and by what we do.

Sometimes our choice is known only by ourselves and God. Sometimes our choices become known by the whole world. Whatever the case, choose we must, and at that point, live with the consequences of that choice.

The third mixture of spices that make up wisdom has to do with teach-ability and blends perfectly with the first two. The ability to listen and learn, the ability to apply that learning to your life, the ability to receive correction and discipline and appreciate it for what it is worth; these are the spices that make up the blend of teach- ability.

There are many lessons that we learn in life. Some are learned from our own experiences, sometimes good and sometimes not so good. Some are learned from watching what happens to others around us. We see the consequences of the actions of our friends and neighbors and learn from them. And still, other lessons are learned from what we are taught from our elders and mentors in life.

Wherever these lessons come from, wisdom is the simple act of applying these lessons to our life and not making the same mistakes. One of life's great lessons was learned when I was about four years old. We lived in the small town of Quinton at the time, and our house sat beside a creek. This creek had a deep bank, maybe twenty or thirty feet deep (actually it was about four or five feet deep, but at four years old, everything is much larger and deeper). It was a beautiful, spring day, and I was out riding the tricycle around the house. It was on my second or third lap when I happened to notice that an old slide had been laid onto the bank of the creek. I got off the tricycle and walked over to investigate further. This was perfect. The top of the slide was lying even with the top of the creek bank, and the bottom flowed seamlessly down to the dry creek bed.

I could see it in my mind: I would ride my tricycle up to the slide, ease it gently over the brink, and then in a blink of an eye, have the ride of my life, coming to a swirling stop in the creek bed.

With the plan in my head, teeth clenched with determination, I eased up to the top of slide. I inched the tricycle over the top, and that is the last thing I remember. My next recollection is that of mom leaning over me to see if I was still alive. Lesson learned: "The best laid schemes of mice and men often go awry," (Robert Burns from *To a Mouse*) a lesson that I have applied over and over again.

What are the lessons that you have learned so far from life? Are you applying them still? Wisdom tells us to be teachable and to learn, whether it be from our own lessons or from the lessons of others. Let this spice be sprinkled across the width and depth of your life.

Another part of this blend is the ability to receive correction and discipline and accept it. And not just accept it, but apply it back into your life. This is probably the most difficult of the spices to use, because it is almost always associated with some kind of pain.

When you were young you received discipline from me and your mother. This discipline was used to teach you the right way to live, respect for yourself and for others, and give you a sense of the rules that you would have to live by when you struck out on your own.

Our discipline for you consisted mainly of setting up rules for the house and expecting you to follow them. Such things as keeping your room picked up and keeping your bathroom clean were where we started. From there we worked on such things as curfews and what to wear (mostly what not to wear). We crossed into discipline for your life at that point: what was acceptable behavior when you were out with friends or on a date. All along the way this correction and discipline was all meant to give you the life skills you would need when you left our home and went out on your own.

Now you have children of your own and are on the other side. You are now the one meeting out the discipline and correction. Always do so with love in your heart and with the long-term goal in mind. As we taught you the discipline you would need to live on your own, so you must teach your children. This spice, although bitter when you first taste it, leaves a long-lasting flavor in your life. If it is applied too heavily, that flavor remains strong and bitter. But if it is applied with a loving hand, gently and evenly across the years, the bitter taste will quickly go away and be replaced with peaceful flavor that will endure.

The final mixture of spice for the recipe for wisdom deals with your relationships with the people around you. As with many other parts of various recipes for life, the first part of this spice mix is a love for people. Now, I'm not talking about those times when you give somebody a hug on the way out the door and say in passing, "Love ya!" What I am talking about is a true and genuine caring for those around you: your neighbors, the people you work with, the members of your church or Sunday school class, as well as your family members and friends. This caring is not an emotion that you have sometimes and other times maybe not so much. This caring comes from your heart and is created in you by God. It is something that you are compelled to share with all those around you and leaves a fulfilled heart every time.

The next part of this mixture is the other side of the love spice, discernment. Strange as it might be, wisdom needs to have a healthy dose of discernment—the ability to see and judge the true, inner person. And in that judgment, when you see such things as pride, arrogance, and in some cases, plain, old evil, your heart must be strong and your spirit with God. This is when you must stand up against these spirits of the world, these spirits of the devil, and take them on in Jesus name. Be careful not to confuse the acts of those spirits and the person in whom these spirits are acting. Lest we forget that this too is a child of God and may only be one step away from finding God in their life. What has been said by many is still true today: "We must hate the sin, but we must love the sinner." This is the blend of love and discernment, and this is what wisdom cries out for.

Finally, in this mixture we add the salt of your word—being faithful to your word and using your word to give good and sound advice.

Salt is a wonderful analogy for your word. Salt basically has two functions; to preserve and to season—to give flavor. Your word, spoken to others, can do exactly the same thing: it can add flavor to a person's life, and it can preserve a person's soul. Wise words to a friend will mean more to them than any gift you could bring, any meal you could prepare, or any amount of money you give. A wise word spoken can save a life. A wise word spoken can prevent a tragedy. A wise word spoken can heal a wounded heart. A wise word spoken—you fill in the blank, for you have, at sometime in your life, heard a wise word from a friend, and it did that for you.

One last thing about your word: always be true and faithful to it. I learned this from my dad, who learned it from his dad, etc, etc. The story is told of my Grandpa Hood who had gone to the bank to borrow money to pay for some doctor bills that they had incurred. After they had talked over the amount of money needed and the payment terms, he shook hands with the banker and the deal was done. No note was signed and no collateral was required. The banker knew that grandpa's word was all he needed to insure the repayment of the loan.

Your word to another person needs to carry that same weight. You don't need to sign a piece of paper to keep your word. You don't have to put up collateral to hold you to your promise. You simply just need to do whatever it is that you have promised. The more you do this, the more it will just become a part of who you are. As well, it will become a part of who your children will be.

Now, having properly mixed all of the ingredients and spices of wisdom together, let's apply it to life. Know God, and put Him first in your life. Trust God in all parts of your life. Know the difference between right and wrong and choose to do right (choose life). Be teachable, accept correction and discipline, and apply it to your life. Love people and always be true to your word. All these things are wisdom in action, wisdom learned and applied. James, the brother of Jesus, wrote this in his letter to his Christian brothers of that day: "Do not merely listen to the word, and so deceive yourself. Do what it says" (James 1:22, NIV).

I would also encourage you at every opportunity to apply Godly wisdom to all that you do and all that you are about. Be a doer not just a listener!

Recipes for Success

> May the Lord answer you when you are in distress; may the name of the God of Jacob protect you. May he send you help from the sanctuary and grant you support from Zion. May He remember all of your sacrifices and accept your burnt offerings. May he give you the desire of your heart and make all of your plans succeed. We will shout for joy when you are victorious and will lift up our banners in the name of our God. May the Lord grant you all your requests.
>
> Psalms 20: 1–5 (NIV)

As much as we would want, there is no magic spice nor is there a single, secret ingredient that we will find in our recipe for success. Unfortunately, Jack has used up all of the magic beans. However, there are a few simple ingredients that we will use to make up our recipe for success.

Ingredient number one: God is our complete supply. In

our recipe for success, the first thing we must understand and apply is that God gives our success. In Paul's second letter to the church in Corinth, he writes: "For God is the one who gives seed to the farmer and then bread to eat. In the same way He will give you many opportunities to do good (succeed), and He will produce a great harvest of righteousness in you" (2 Corinthians 9:10, NLT).

This was an amazing revelation that God gave to me. His provision is not just the bread that is on my table (my day to day success), but also the seed that produces the harvest that puts the bread on my table (my ability to go out and succeed). God provides it all! My daily successes are provided by God, and my future successes are being planted today by God. As I walk closer with God, He will lead me down the pathways of success. It is my job to always remember to give Him the glory. In Matthew's gospel, Jesus tells us to seek God first in our life, and He will provide for all of our needs—He will give us success. (Matthew 6:33) Success is always found first in God and in His provision to us.

Ingredient number two: the law of the harvest. There is a basic law of seed planting and harvesting and is as follows: You harvest what you plant, you harvest it later than you planted it, and you always harvest more than you planted.

Take for instance, corn: a farmer goes out and plants one seed of corn into the ground. He waters and fertilizes the seed until it sprouts. Soon after that, the stalk begins to produce ears of corn. Each ear of corn now contains hundreds of seeds of corn that can also be planted. Following the analogy above, the farmer planted corn and that is what he got. It took some time for the corn to grow so his harvest was much later than the planting. The farmer also harvested abundantly more than the one seed of corn he originally planted.

Success follows this same law. Whatever you plant in life: that you will also harvest. If you plant due diligence and hard work you will harvest the reward for that work. As well, if you plant seeds of laziness and deceit, your harvest will be thin and poor. The saying is very true that you can't go out and sow your wild oats and then pray for a crop failure.

The key to this ingredient is the seed that you plant. As with fruits and vegetables, there are many different seeds that you can plant and each will produce many different results in your life. When you plant seeds of love, you will get love returned to you. Seeds of respect and trust planted in your husband will be returned many times more. Plant seeds of happiness in your home and neighborhood, and you will live in happiness wherever you are.

In Paul's letter to the church in Galatia, he talks to the church about the fruit that God will produce in them: love, joy, peace patience, kindness, goodness, faithfulness, gentleness, and self-control. All of these fruits come from the seeds that were planted in their lives by God. Paul is encouraging them to continue to water and fertilize this good fruit in them and spread these seeds among all of their friends and family.

In this recipe for success in life, be careful what seeds you plant along the way. Whatever it is that you have planted, somewhere in the future, you will have to bring in that harvest.

The third ingredient that must be added for this recipe for success is giving, and specifically tithing. Yes, I have used the "T" word. For some it would have been better for me to have written some profanity or curse word than to read the "T" word, but I am going to explain to you why this is also necessary for your recipe for success.

In all the many passages and stories of the Bible, there is more time dedicated to the issue of giving than anything else. Jesus talked about it often, as does Paul and the other writers of the New Testament. Therefore, if God spends that much time talking about it (giving and tithing), it must be important, and we must add this ingredient to our recipe for success.

Sugar, Spice, and Lessons for Life

God knows that all of our adult life is consumed by earning a living for ourselves and for our family, and that is why He spends so much time talking about money, finances, and giving in His word. So, let's see what God has to tell us about this very important ingredient.

The prophet Malachi wrote this to the people of Israel in his day: "'Bring all the tithes into the storehouse so there will be enough food in my Temple. If you do,' says the Lord Almighty. 'I will open the windows of heaven for you. I will pour out a blessing so great you won't have enough room to take it in! Try it! Let me prove it to you!'" (Malachi 3:10, NLT)

In this word to the people of Israel, God was telling them to give Him and His way a try. Just like we go out and test drive a car before we buy it, God is telling the people to just try this out. Give God's way a test drive, and see if it works. God's promise to them and to you is that He will honor your obedience and pour out a blessing from heaven that you will not have enough room to hold. This blessing is specifically in reference to your material possessions and your success. The book of Malachi is the last book of the Old Testament. Read what God's promises are in the 3rd chapter for those who will obey Him. All of these promises start with the simple act of giving back to God the first 10% of all that He has given to you. Seem too simple? God's word: "Let me prove it to you!"

Jesus also taught about giving. In Luke's gospel, he records these words from Jesus: "If you give, you will receive. Your gift will return to you in full measure, pressed down, shaken together to make room for more, and running over. Whatever measure you use in giving—large or small—it will be used to measure what is given back to you," (Luke 6:38, NLT).

If we give in small cups, our return will be in small cups. If we give in buckets, it will be returned to us in buckets. If we give in barrels, it will be returned to us in barrels. Whatever measurement we use to give, that will be the measurement used to return it back to us. This applies to all parts of our life, not just the financial. Anything that we give: our time, our efforts, our energy, our home, our love, our patience, our kindness, our trust, etc; all will be returned back to us. The amount that is returned is progressively more than the amount that we give. As we give more, we are given more, which in turn allows us to give more, from which we are given even more... I think you can see how this easily multiplies. The simple truth is that you can't out-give God.

There are many, many more examples and numerous scriptures that God gives to us about giving. I will let you search these out for yourself. God tells us that to be successful we are to give; give to God the first 10% of all that He has given to us and to give generously to all who need. If we do this, God promises success in our life.

The last ingredient of the recipe for success to be added is plain, old work ethic. There is no more tried and true ingredient to success that you can add. Nor is there a more satisfying way to success.

Many quotes and anecdotes have been spoken and written across the years about success, but the two that ring truest to me are: "The harder I work, the luckier I get," (Samuel Goldwyn). And, along with that quote is: "Luck is where preparation (hard work) meets opportunity," (Author Unknown). Both of these quotes point out the obvious... there is no such thing as luck and that hard work will create its own opportunities.

The problem that most people have with hard work is that it is hard. You have to start at the bottom and work through each step and each level to reach your full potential. In a world today that demands instant everything and all things available at the push of a button, this concept seems far outdated. A young person right out of school expects a job with a corner office and a six figure income. If that is not readily available (and it is not), they often retreat back to home, or perhaps back to school for a graduate degree. If they can just hold out long enough, surely these HR people will wake up and see what their true potential and worth to this company would be!

You have already seen that this is just not true. Getting to the top of anything requires starting at the bottom and climbing your way up. This is true in the business world, and it is true in all other aspects of life. Success is not handed to a person on a silver platter. It must be sought after and worked for. Whatever it is that you are striving for—a new position at work, learning anything, becoming the best mother and wife you can be; it will take your best effort to become the best you can be.

A second piece of this hard work ingredient is planning. You've no doubt heard the saying that people don't plan to fail, they just fail to plan, and I believe that is correct. The amount of hard work that you put in every day is inversely proportional to the amount of planning you do. The better the plan, the less hard the work will be. The less you plan, the harder and longer you have to work.

Jesus told his disciples to consider the cost before building a tower. In other words, make a plan before you go to work and consider all of the work to be done before you get started. That way you won't get half way through the job and have to quit.

A friend of mine said it this way: "Always remember the seven "Ps" to a good job—prior, proper planning prevents pitifully, poor performance." It is the first three "Ps" that are the key: Prior, Proper Planning. Make a plan, and then go work the plan. Success is not too far behind.

One other integral part of the hard work ingredient is this: don't give up! There are going to be times

Sugar, Spice, and Lessons for Life

when it seems that you will never reach your goal. Don't give up! There will be times when you will want to quit. Don't give up! There will be times when you will question yourself and all of your decisions. Don't give up! There will be times that it is just too hard to go on. Don't give up!

There was a college basketball coach, Jimmy Valvano, who coached at North Carolina State. He led an unlikely group of players to a national championship back in the 80s. They were under-dogs through the whole tournament, but through persistence and hard work they won the title. It was not too many years after their win that Coach Valvano was diagnosed with cancer. He held on bravely for a just a few months. In the last speech he would give just a few short days before he passed on, he left his team and the world with this final exhortation: "Don't give up. Don't ever give up!"

So, let's now combine all of these ingredients for our recipe for success:

Acknowledge God as your compete supply

Plant good seeds, and expect a good harvest

Give generously first to God and then to all who need

Work hard, plan well, and don't ever give up

Put all of these ingredients into practice in your life, and you will be successful in all you do.

Recipes for the Proverbs 31 Woman

A wife of noble character who can find? She is worth far more than rubies. Her husband has full confidence in her and lacks nothing of value. She brings him good, not harm, all the days of her life. She selects wool and flax and works with eager hands. She is like the merchant ships, bringing her food from afar. She gets up while it is still night; she provides food for her family and portions for her women servants. She considers a field and buys it; out of her earnings she plants a vineyard. She sets about her work vigorously; her arms are strong for her tasks. She sees that her trading is profitable, and her lamp does not go out at night. In her hand she holds the distaff and grasps the spindle with her fingers. She opens her arms to the poor and extends her hands to the needy. When it snows, she has no fear for her household; for all of them are clothed in scarlet. She makes coverings for her bed; she is clothed in fine linen and purple. Her husband is respected at the city gate, where he takes his seat among the elders of the land. She makes linen garments and sells them, and supplies the merchants with sashes. She is clothed with strength and dignity; she can laugh at the days to come. She speaks with wisdom, and faithful instruction is on her tongue. She watches over the affairs of her household and does not eat the bread of idleness. Her children arise and call her blessed; her husband also, and he praises her: "Many women do noble things, but you surpass them all." Charm is deceptive, and beauty is fleeting; but a woman who fears the Lord is to be praised. Honor her for all that her hands have done, and let her works bring her praise at the city gate.

Proverbs 31: 10–31, NIV

So just who is this superhuman woman that is being described here? June Cleaver on steroids? Is she a cross between Claire Huxtable and Carol Brady with just a pinch of Sharon Osbourne? Is there one person who has all of the characteristics mentioned in Proverbs 31? The simple answer is *no*! If that lady ever had lived, she would have been assassinated about two days after she moved into the neighborhood. So do we just write this off as an impossible recipe to make in your life? Once again, the simple answer is *no*! Let's just break this down into some smaller portions that are easier to handle at one sitting, and perhaps at the end of this recipe, it can be combined into something that you can work into your life.

The first main ingredient in this woman's life is hard work (seems like I've mentioned this before, huh?). "A man may work from sun to sun, but a woman's work is never done." You've heard that before, I'm sure. But what is that little rhyme actually saying about a Proverbs 31 woman? I see three key ingredients in this first part of the recipe: provides food for her family, provides clothes for her family, and is a smart businesswoman.

Providing food for your family; there is nothing really difficult in the interpretations of this piece of the ingredients. This is simply your actions to make sure that your husband and children are fed well, and no, that does not mean that you have to prepare a sixteen course meal for them every time they sit down at the table. However, this does mean that you have to put together a good and nutritious meal for them. Do you have to personally prepare this meal, working for hours on end in the kitchen? Not necessarily, if you have the available funds to order in or have everybody ready to go out for that meal. The issue is having a plan for that meal and seeing it through to completion. Whether you prepare it yourself, or buy it ready to eat, have your family meals ready.

Another couple of thoughts on the family meals: as best as you can, make it a happy and enjoyable time and work hard to have all of your family sit down together at least once a day for a meal together. Let me explain further…

Your meals together should be, as best as you can make them, a happy and enjoyable time. There is nothing worse for a family and for the individuals of that family to have a fight during a meal. I know you have seen it before, and the consequences of a fight during meal time are many. Some of these consequences are ulcers, acid reflux, and other digestive problems; emotional issues that cause eating disorders, long term bad eating habits that cause weight issues, and the list goes on. I would encourage you to set a family rule stating that all major discussions should take place away from the meal times. You can even go as far as setting aside a time and place for them to happen if you need. By doing this, meal time will be a great memory for you and for your children, and you will also set for them a great example to follow in their lives to come.

Your meals together also should be eaten together. Sounds kind of silly when you say it that way, but it is really just that simple. Families that eat at least one meal a day together, generally speaking, will have fewer of the large issues to deal with as their children grow up. This seems to be a largely accepted principle among most family therapists. Having a meal together as a family solidifies the bonds that you have; it brings security to the family and can become a time where love and trust are shared equally.

The second ingredient in the "hard work" part of this recipe is providing clothing for your family.

In years past, (many, many years past) this meant that a woman would sit at a sewing machine for hours or perhaps sit with knitting needles or crochet hooks, making all of her family's clothes by hand. These skills are now only hobbies, and in that, only for a few women who have the time to do them. I see this ingredient as a process of making sure that your family is dressed appropriately for whatever the conditions or occasions might bring.

I see this also as making sure that the clothes your family wears are neat, clean, and fit correctly. How your family looks is truly a direct reflection on you. A family who looks good and is dressed correctly is usually seen with a mother and wife who looks just as good. As well, we have all seen the opposite family who are dressed in dirty, torn clothes that do not fit and the mother and wife almost always is dressed just the same. Take the time to send your husband and children out into the world dressed well. Everybody will notice, whether they say so or not.

The third and last ingredient in the "hard work" part of this recipe is being a smart businesswoman. You just thought that not going to an office every day got you out this responsibility. Let's look at how this is a part of your everyday life.

What "business" decisions does the average wife and mother make each day? First you have to make up a spending plan for your family's income: how much is being spent on the monthly bills, and then how much is available for food, clothing, entertainment, etc. This requires the same skills as a corporate, financial manager or accountant.

Next, you have to be able to be a skillful purchaser; knowing the difference between a truly good buy and just another sale. A skillful purchaser also watches for the best time to buy certain products to get the biggest bang for her buck. Buying clothes on sale or during the off-season can make a huge difference in your spending plan. A skillful purchaser also has great negotiation skills. The ability to get what you want and get it at the price you want to pay; this is an art that few people possess. The job requirements for a corporate purchasing agent fall into all of these categories.

You also need to have a shrewd business sense. Now, what do I mean by that? Simply put, you need to be able to sniff out a con. From the man selling vacuums door to door, to your child telling you that the puppy just followed him home, you need to know when you are being conned. This is more of a sixth sense than something that you learn. There are always certain things to look out for, and this can be learned, but intuition plays a much larger roll in this ability. If it walks like a duck, looks like a duck, and quacks like a duck... it must be a duck! Don't doubt yourself. If you were wrong, no harm done. But if you were right, how much time, money, or pain did you just save yourself and your family? A corporate CEO or president is the person you see with these kinds of abilities.

Finally, put with all of these skills the ability to manage people—your family. Settling disputes over work duties, making payroll (allowances), hearing grievances, and making the final decision, all of these are a part of the day to day work of both a wife and mother and the corporate director of human resources.

It would seem to me that the saying is very true: "The hand that rocks the cradle rules the world."

The second main ingredient in this recipe for the Proverbs 31 woman is generosity. Once again, this may ring a bell with you from an earlier chapter, and yes, we are going to talk about it again, although giving and being generous are not the same. Let's first take a look at what separates the two.

Being generous is the spirit in which all giving takes place. However, a person can give without being generous. Giving can take place because of guilt or because of a sense of compulsion (being made to give), or because of high emotion (maybe a tragedy has created a need). Being generous is what motivates a person to give of themselves, of their money, of their time, or of their energies on a day to day basis. Being generous is a character trait, not an action. It is who you are, not what you do.

The Proverbs 31 woman is generous with her finances and gives to the local church and charities. She is generous with her skill and will donate a portion of the work of her hands. She is generous with her time and will make herself available for her friends, her family, and her neighbors. She is generous with her love, giving to all who are in need.

Generosity is a part of this recipe, because at its heart is true love. Love for your family, love for your neighbors, and love for all those in need. If this were left out of the recipe, it would be left flat and without much flavor. Having a generous heart gives flavor to not only your life, but to all those around you. Your children watch you and learn. Your husband watches you and is proud. And, the people you help watch you and receive the love that comes from your acts of generosity. All of this adds spice and flavor to your life as a Proverbs 31 woman and to all of the recipes of your life.

Pressing on in this recipe for the Proverbs 31 woman, we must add the necessary ingredient of wisdom, and not just ordinary wisdom, but wisdom with a good measure of intellect. Now intellect is not just confined to book smarts or college degrees. Intellect is the accumulation of learning from any number of sources. Learning may come from a formal education in college, it may come from the life that you have lived, or it may come from observing others and the consequences of their choices.

It is this combination of intellect (from school and from life) and wisdom that the Proverbs 31 woman applies to her decisions and her choices throughout her life. It is what separates her from other women who spend their time making foolish choices and poor decisions. It is what defines her as a strong woman. It is a large part of what makes her husband proud and gives him reason to trust her with the day to day decisions of running their household.

Finally, we add the essential ingredient of faith and trust in God. All of the previous ingredients really add up to just a bunch of stuff unless it is held together with the oil of the Holy Spirit of God. All that you do and all that you are must be wrapped up and held together in God. Without God, all of this really adds up to just a bunch of work, money, time, and effort thrown down the drain. However, with God, all of your work has meaning, all of your giving is multiplied, all of your love is increased, and all of your wisdom is endowed. With God, all things are possible, and any challenge can be met and overcome. With God you can be the Proverbs 31 woman!

The Proverbs 31 woman is a recipe that can be applied to your life. Perhaps it will come together quickly, or perhaps it will come together over a lifetime. But if you will allow God to work in your life every day, this recipe can and will be prepared and the dish served will be wonderful.

Recipes for Happiness

Rejoice in the Lord always. I will say it again, rejoice! Let your gentleness be evident to all. The Lord is near. Do not be anxious about anything, but in everything, by prayer and petition, with thanksgiving, present your requests to God. And the peace of God which transcends all understanding will guard your hearts and your minds in Christ Jesus. Finally, brothers, whatever is true, whatever is noble, whatever is right, whatever is pure, whatever is lovely, whatever is admirable—if anything is excellent or praiseworthy—think about such things. Whatever you have learned or received or heard from me—put it into practice. And the God of peace will be with you. I know what it is to be in need, and I know what it is to have plenty. I have learned the secret of

> being content in any and every situation, whether well fed or hungry, whether living in plenty or in want. I can do everything through Him who gives me strength. And my God will meet all your needs according to His glorious riches in Christ Jesus.
>
> Philippians 4: 4–9, 12–13, 19, NIV

I thought it appropriate to wrap up this recipe book with a recipe that is all too often not prepared. Many people, for whatever reason, either do not know how or do not want to know how to prepare this recipe. That is why I wanted to give this recipe to you. Above all things in this world, I wish for you happiness, and I wanted to pass on to you a recipe that was given to me many years ago.

In this passage from Paul's letter to the church in Philippi, he gives them a recipe for happiness. This recipe, taken from the passage above is as follows:

1. Be content in any and every situation, whether living in need or living in wealth.

2. Dwell on good things, things that are true, things that are noble, things that are right, things that are pure, things that are lovely, things that are admirable, things that are excellent, and things that are praiseworthy.

3. Don't worry about anything, but pray about everything, and trust God for all of your answers to these prayers.

4. Acknowledge that you can do all things through Christ who gives you strength.

5. Know that God will meet all of your needs according to His wealth, not according to yours

When we define happiness at its foundation is the word: contentment. Paul, in this letter to the church at Philippi, makes the statement that he has learned how to be content in every situation that he is in, whether well fed or hungry, whether living in luxury or in poverty. To give context to his statement, you should know that he was writing this letter from a prison cell in Rome. This prison cell was not what you would see in today's modern prison, it was more of a cave, carved out of the earth underneath the city. It was dark, wet, smelly, nasty with human filth and dead bodies, and you were held in chains. It was from that place Paul made the statement that he had learned to be content, and to be happy in every situation.

Whatever our present situation might be (and it certainly could not be any worse than Paul's), we need to learn to be content there. I've lived in a number of places, both big and small, and I can also tell you that the first key ingredient to happiness is to be content wherever you are. When we lived in Texas, I was never content with the life that I had there, and consequently, it was a very difficult time for me. Even though we prospered financially, I was never content while living down there.

I have lived in a number of other places since then, and I have learned what it is to find contentment, and to find happiness, wherever I am living. It is a choice, a choice that we make in the midst of the circumstances in which we live: I will be content, I will be happy! When you can say this along with Paul in every situation, you will have found true contentment.

Positive thinking has, in the past, taken a bad rap. Granted it was way overused in the 80s by any number of happiness gurus and televangelists, but God tells us to think on positive things, and this is the second ingredient in our recipe for happiness.

Paul said it this way in the New Living Translation: "Fix your thoughts on what is true and honorable and right. Think about things that are pure and lovely and admirable. Think about things that are excellent and worthy of praise" (Philippians 4:8, NLT). In a nutshell, think about positive things.

You should spend your time dwelling on the good in people, and the good that they do. Think about times when a person has done something good. Consider truth, honor, and righteousness in your family, friends, and neighbors. By spending your time focused on good and positive things, your attitude immediately reflects those same happy feelings.

Now I am not telling you to walk around with your head in the clouds, oblivious to the world around you. What I am telling you is that if you put good thoughts in your mind through the day, happiness will be the result in your life. God tells us to be positive thinkers, so be happy!

The next ingredient works hand in hand with the ingredient of happiness: don't worry. Yes, that song is going through my mind right now too. "Don't worry, be happy." Now I'm not talking about the kind of "don't worry" that has your head in the clouds looking for every silver lining. There is another kind of "don't worry" that we read about in the bible, and that is what we want to look at.

Paul tells you to not worry about anything but rather to pray about everything. Let God know what your needs are, and then trust Him to take care of them. By doing this, God will give you a sense of peace and happiness that is only found in Him. The hard part of this is not the praying part—talking to God and letting Him know how you feel. The hard part is the letting go of the problem, placing it into God's hands and letting Him solve the problem. And, along with letting God solve the problem, trusting that His solution is the best way to go.

How much time is spent worrying about things that never come to pass? How much energy is spent on trying to find a solution to a problem that God already has fixed? How much happiness is lost when we forget that we have a loving God who cares for even the smallest detail of your life? If we will take all of our worries to God, He has promised to take care of them, and He will!

As we continue on with this recipe for happiness, the next ingredient that is added is the substance from which the last two ingredients were taken. Acknowledging that I can do anything and everything through the strength given to me by Christ Jesus takes away any need for worry and replaces it with positive and productive thoughts.

That statement: "I can do all things through Christ who gives me strength," (Philippians 4:13, NIV), is perhaps the largest and most dynamic statement in God's word. The freedom and happiness brought about by knowing that you can handle whatever the world has to throw at you is immeasurable. It is, however, the clause "through Christ" that fills your heart with peace, knowing that you are never alone in the battle. It is "through Christ" that you can do all things.

"Through Christ" - you can handle all the problems of life and the finality of death. "Through Christ" - you can manage to work a dead-end job. "Through Christ" - you can be a caring mother to your children and a loving wife to your husband. "Through Christ" - you can face all of life's adversities. "Through Christ" - you are happy and free from worry.

Finally, in this recipe for happiness, we add the surety that the same God that has taken care of me and all of my needs over the past many years (almost 50 now!) will also supply all of the needs that you have from His riches in heaven, given to us through Jesus Christ. What level of happiness is brought by knowing that whatever our need might be, God will fill that need.

This wraps up all of the ingredients mentioned above with the love of God found only through Jesus Christ. Contentment, positive thoughts, not worrying, and acknowledging that through Christ you can do anything, are all wrapped up in a loving and caring God who will take care of every need that you have. This is truly the ultimate gift, and it gives you the ultimate happiness. A happiness that is from God and through God and reflects God in all that you do.

A Last Bite

"A final word: Be strong with Lord's mighty power. Put on God's armor so that you will be able to stand firm against all strategies and tricks of the Devil"

(Ephesians 6: 10–11, NIV).

So what has this recipe book been all about, cute stories and references between life and cooking? Has it been just another long sermon similar to the ones I would bring to you when you were growing up?

I would hope that this book will give you not just food for the kitchen, but also food for your life. You are now a woman, a wife, and a mother with all of the responsibilities of each one. To survive in this world, you will need help and strength; the kind that only God can provide. Your mother and I will be there for you whenever you need, but our resources are limited, whereas the resources of God are limitless and endless.

My purpose for writing this book has been to give you a few of these recipes that will direct you to the endless supply that God has for you. Long after your mother and I are gone from this world, God will still be with you, taking care of every need that you have. These recipes for life are to direct you into His love, His grace, His wisdom, His will, His success, and His happiness. It is my prayer that you will become twice the chef that I ever was, in the kitchen and in life.

Recipes for the Kitchen

81   Helpful Cooking Tips

84   Appetizers and Salads

93   Vegetables and Side Dishes

99   Main Course

127   Desserts

Helpful Cooking Tips

1. Do not put your face over a pot or pan when removing the lid.
2. Always wear a shirt when frying bacon.
3. A tablespoon is not the dirty spoon left on the table.
4. Do not try to catch a dropped knife.
5. Do not put aluminum foil in the microwave oven.
6. Do not put plastic wrap in the conventional oven.

7. Boiling water is hot (212 degrees); handle with care.

8. Do not put potato peels down the garbage disposal.

9. Do not put eating utensils into the garbage disposal.

10. One cup does not equal one coffee cup.

11. Do not put a spoon into the blender when in operation.

12. Do not put a knife into a toaster to dislodge a piece of toast or bagel while it is still plugged in.

13. Do not slice potatoes or anything else while holding it in your hand.

14. For better baked potatoes from the microwave, wrap them in wax paper.

15. For day-old donuts, cover them with a slightly damp paper towel and cook in the microwave for 10 seconds.

16. Do not put water on a grease fire, use baking soda or flour or an appropriate fire extinguisher

17. Do not put hot grease in a plastic cup (it will melt).

18. Anything found in the fridge that is green and fuzzy should be thrown away.

19. Anything found with an expiration date of one year or older should only be handled by the local hazmat team.

20. In the event of any cooking emergencies, do not call mom, she will only ask silly questions and then hand the phone over to me.

Taco Salad

- 1 ½ pound hamburger meat
- 1 package McKormicks taco seasoning
- 1 can kidney beans
- 1 cup grated cheese
- 1 container shredded lettuce
- 1 box large taco shells
- 1 jar picante sauce

Brown hamburger meat and drain fat. Add package of taco seasoning and the required amount of water according to the package directions. Let simmer for fifteen minutes. Place this mixture in a container and chill for two hours. In a large taco shell, put lettuce, drained kidney beans, chilled taco meat, cheese, and top with picante sauce.

Chicken Pasta Salad

- 4 pieces boneless/skinless chicken breasts
- 1 package bowtie pasta
- 1 onion
- 1 green pepper
- 1 red pepper
- 1 bottle zesty Italian salad dressing
- 1 container parmesan cheese

In one large pot, add bowtie pasta to boiling water and boil for twelve to fifteen minutes until tender. In another large pot, add chicken breast to boiling water and boil for thirty minutes. Drain pasta and pour into large bowel. Cut chicken into small pieces and add to pasta. Dice ½ of onion, green pepper, and red pepper and stir into pasta. Stir in one cup of zesty Italian dressing and one cup parmesan cheese (add more to taste if needed). Chill for two hours and serve.

Tuna Salad

- 2 cans of tuna
- ½ cup of grated cheese
- 1 bottle of Catalina salad dressing
- Lettuce

Drain juice from cans of tuna and crumble over shredded lettuce. Add grated cheese and Catalina salad dressing to taste. Serve immediately.

Nachos

- 1 package tortilla chips
- 1 package grated—cheddar, Monterrey jack or a blend of both

Options as follows:
- 1 cup sliced jalapeno peppers
- ½ cup of onions
- 1 diced tomato
- 1 cup diced chicken (pre-cooked)
- 1 cup refried beans
- ½ cup sliced black olives
- Picante sauce
- Sour Cream

Place the chips on a large, baking sheet and cover with grated cheese. Add any of the options mentioned above and bake in a pre-heated oven at 350 degrees for ten to twelve minutes until the cheese is completely melted. Serve with picante sauce and sour cream on the side.

Rotel Queso Dip

- 2 cans Rotel tomatoes and peppers
- 1 package Velveeta cheese

Soften Velveeta cheese in microwave oven until fairly liquid. Add two cans Rotel and mix thoroughly. Microwave on high for about two more minutes to heat all the way through. Stir again and serve with tortilla chips or any other chip or cracker.

Homemade Salsa

- 1 10 ounce can diced tomatoes and green chilies, un-drained
- 1 tablespoon seeded and chopped jalapeno pepper
- 1 tablespoon chopped red onion
- 1 tablespoon minced, fresh cilantro
- 1 garlic clove, minced
- 1 tablespoon olive oil
- Dash of salt
- Dash of pepper
- Tortilla chips

In a small bowl, combine the tomatoes, jalapeno, onion, cilantro, garlic, oil, salt and pepper. Refrigerate until serving. Serve with tortilla chips.

When you are cutting or seeding hot peppers, use rubber or plastic gloves to protect your hands. Avoid touching your face or eyes.

Potato Salad

- 6 to 8 medium potatoes
- 1 cup mayonaisse
- ½ cup of mustard
- 1 cup sweet pickle relish
- 4 eggs—hard boiled and diced
- 1 medium onion, diced

Slice potatoes into small chunks and boil until soft. Drain water and put into mixing bowl with all other ingredients. Mix together with electric, hand blender and chill for about two hours.

Green Bean Casserole

- 3 cans French style green beans
- 2 cans cream of mushroom soup
- 1 can dried onion rings

Drain water from green beans and mix with cream of mushroom soup and ½ a can of dried onion rings. Pour mixture into baking dish and sprinkle remaining dried onion rings on top. Bake at 350 degrees for thirty minutes

Fried Okra, Zucchini, or Squash

- As much as you want to eat of either okra, zucchini, or squash
- 4 eggs
- ½ cup milk
- Salt
- Pepper
- Italian Spice
- Flour
- Corn Meal

Mix eggs and milk in bowl and set to one side.

Mix 1 cup flour, ½ cup corn meal, 1 tablespoon Italian Spice, 2 teaspoons salt, and 1 teaspoon pepper in a bowl with a fork to evenly distribute all ingredients and set to one side.

Wash vegetables and dunk into egg mixture. Take out of egg mixture and dredge through the flour mixture. Place in skillet with 4 tablespoons olive oil, on medium to medium high heat and cook until golden brown.

Zesty Mashed Potatoes

- 6–8 medium potatoes
- ½ cup milk
- 1 stick butter or margarine
- ½ cup ranch dressing
- 2 tablespoons salt
- 1 tablespoon pepper

Slice potatoes into small chunks and boil until tender. Drain and pour into mixing bowl with all of the other ingredients. Mix with a hand blender to desired consistency.

Aunt Missy's Green Beans

- 2 cans green beans
- 2 tablespoons of oil
- ½ cup of sugar

In skillet, put in oil and green beans. Cook until beans are lightly browned. Add sugar and cook for addition ten minutes until all sugar is melted, stirring frequently.

Baked Beans

- 2 cans pork and beans
- ½ cup diced onions
- ½ cup barbeque sauce
- ½ cup ketchup
- ½ cup brown sugar
- 1 tablespoon mustard
- 3–4 strips of bacon

Preheat oven to 350 degrees. Drain juice from pork & beans and combine all ingredients. Lay strips of bacon on top and bake for one hour.

Fried Bologna

- 1 package bologna
- 1 tablespoon oil

In a skillet, pour in oil and coat bottom. Place two slices of bologna in skillet and slice hole in middle to allow for release of steam. Grill until browned. Serve on sandwich bread with any of the following: cheese, mustard, onion, etc.

Porcupine Meatballs

- 1 pound hamburger meat
- 1 box Rice-A-Roni Beef Flavor
- 1 jar brown gravy

Combine hamburger meat with Rice-A-Roni in a large bowl, let stand for thirty minutes. Roll into small to medium balls and cook in skillet for twenty-five to thirty minutes, stirring to brown all sides of the meat ball and drain fat. Pour brown gravy on top and simmer for fifteen minutes.

Serve over mashed potatoes, noodles, or rice (noodles and rice—follow directions on packages).

Baked Chicken with Rice

- 2–4 pieces boneless/skinless chicken breasts
- 2 boxes Rice-A-Roni (1 chicken flavor, 1 broccoli & cheese)
- 2 cans cream of chicken soup
- 2 cups water

Preheat oven to 350 degrees. In a baking dish, pour in Rice-A-Roni, water, and chicken soups, stirring all together. Lay chicken breasts on top and bake uncovered for one hour.

Chicken Fried Steak

- 2–4 pieces tenderized round steak
- 4 eggs
- 1 cup milk
- 2 cups flour
- 2 teaspoons salt
- 2 teaspoons pepper
- 2–4 tablespoons oil

In a bowl, combine eggs and milk and stir until blended. In another bowl, combine flour, salt, and pepper and stir together. Pour oil into skillet and cover bottom. Dip each piece of steak into egg and milk mixture, and then dredge into the flour mixture. Fry in skillet, turning over to brown both sides and cook for about fifteen minutes.

For gravy, add about two tablespoons of oil to remaining drippings in skillet. Sprinkle two to three large tablespoons of flour into skillet, and stir until all is mixed together and is browning. Add two cups of milk to this and stir until thickened. If mixture is too thick, add another cup of milk and continue to stir.

For mashed potatoes, peel and slice six medium to large potatoes and put into pot of boiling water. Boil for ten minutes until potatoes are tender. Drain water and add one stick butter, and one cup milk. Mix with blender until soft. For added flavor to potatoes, add one cup Ranch Dressing.

Hamburger Steak with Grilled Onions

- 2–4 hamburger patties
- 1 chopped onion
- 2 tablespoons oil
- 2 tablespoons garlic

In a skillet, pour oil and add chopped onions. Sauté for five minutes while stirring frequently. Place hamburger patties in with the onions and continue cooking. Sprinkle garlic on both sides of patties as they are cooking. Serve with chips or french fries.

Sloppy Joes

- 1 ½ pound hamburger meat
- 1 package McKormicks Sloppy Joe mix
- 1 large can tomato sauce
- 1 can rotel
- ½ cup ketchup
- ½ cup barbeque sauce
- ½ cup brown sugar
- 1 teaspoon hot sauce
- ½ cup chopped onion
- 1 cup water

Brown hamburger meat with onion and drain fat. Combine all other ingredients and mix completely. Simmer for fifteen to twenty minutes. Serve on toasted buns with cheese or Rotel cheese dip.

Chili

- 2 pounds coarse ground chili meat
- 1 package Wick Fowlers Chili Seasoning mix
- 1 onion chopped
- 1 large can tomato sauce
- 1 can Rotel
- ¼ cup sliced jalapeno peppers
- 1 tablespoon garlic
- 2 tablespoons salt
- 2 bottles of beer
- ½ cup of sugar

Brown chili meat with chopped onion and drain fat. In large pot, combine all ingredients (except beer) and stir together. Add browned chili meat and onion to large pot. Add one bottle of beer and stir together. Let simmer for one to two hours. (If you are cooking chili all day, add 2nd bottle of beer after about three hours of cooking).

Serve with Jiffy Corn Bread (follow box directions), Fritos Corn Chips, or Ritz Crackers, and Grated Cheese.

Mexican Dish

- 1 ½ pound hamburger meat
- 1 can refried beans
- 1 package McKormicks burrito seasoning
- 1 large can tomato sauce
- ½ cup water
- ½ cup sugar
- 1 tablespoon garlic
- 1 tablespoon chili powder
- 2 boxes Jiffy cornbread mix (follow directions on box)

Preheat oven to 350 degrees. Mix cornbread and pour into greased pan.

Cook cornbread for fifteen minutes and remove from oven. Brown hamburger and drain fat from pan. Add all remaining ingredients and simmer for ten minutes.

Pour hamburger mix on top of cornbread and cover with grated cheese. Bake in oven for twenty-five minutes. Serve with picante sauce and chips.

Burritos

- ½ pound hamburger meat
- 1 can refried beans
- 1 package McKormicks Burrito mix
- 1 large can tomato sauce
- 1 tablespoon garlic
- ½ cup water

Options
- Grated cheese
- Sour cream
- Chopped onion
- Chopped black olives
- Chopped tomatoes
- Chopped lettuce
- Picante sauce

Brown hamburger meat and drain fat. Add other in other ingredients and simmer for fifteen minutes.

Serve with any of the above options in either a soft flour tortilla or crispy taco shells.

Chicken Enchiladas

- 1 package flour tortillas
- 2 cans chicken
- 3 cans cream of chicken soup
- 1 large package sour cream
- 2 cups grated cheese

Combine two cans of chicken, two cans cream of chicken soup, sour cream, and one cup grated cheese, mixing together completely. Roll this mixture into the flour tortillas and place in a greased baking pan. In a separate bowl, combine the remaining can of cream of chicken soup and one cup grated cheese. Pour this over the enchiladas in the baking pan. Cook in preheated oven at 350 degrees for fifteen to twenty minutes.

Serve with picante sauce, chips, and jalapenos.

Spaghetti Sauce

- 1 ½ pound hamburger meat
- 1 package McKormicks Spaghetti Seasoning mix
- 1 large can tomato sauce
- 1 small can tomato paste
- 1 tablespoon garlic
- 2 tablespoons Italian seasoning
- ½ cup sugar
- 1 cup water

Brown hamburger and drain fat. Add all other ingredients and simmer for fifteen minutes.

In large pot of boiling water, add two tablespoons of oil and one tablespoon of salt. Add spaghetti noodles and boil for twelve to fifteen minutes, stirring frequently until tender.

Spaghetti Sauce No Meat

- 1 onion chopped
- 1 cup wine
- 1 can Rotel
- 1 can tomato sauce
- 1 package McKormicks Spaghetti Sauce mix
- ½ cup sugar
- 2 tablespoons oil
- 1 package parmesan cheese

In a skillet, pour oil and coat bottom, add chopped onion, and sauté for ten minutes, stirring frequently. Drain excess oil and add remaining ingredients except parmesan cheese. Simmer for 20 minutes, stirring frequently. Serve over spaghetti noodles and finish with sprinkle of parmesan cheese.

Lasagna

- Spaghetti sauce (same as in previous recipes)
- 16 lasagna noodles
- 1 container cottage cheese
- 1 cup of each type of cheese
    - Cheddar
    - Mozzarella
    - Parmesan

Preheat oven to 350 degrees. Boil lasagna noodles for ten minutes. In a greased, baking dish, put four lasagna noodles in bottom, cover lightly with spaghetti sauce, cottage cheese, and three cheese mixture. Repeat procedure for the next three layers. Cover top layer of noodles with sauce and three cheese mixture only. Bake in oven for thirty minutes.

Serve with hot bread sticks or a loaf of French bread.

Pizza Bake

- 1 can Grands biscuits
- Spaghetti sauce (same as in previous recipes)
- 1 cup grated cheese

   Options
   - 1 can mushrooms
   - ½ cup chopped onion
   - ½ cup chopped green pepper
   - ½ cup chopped pepperoni
   - ½ cup sliced black olives

Preheat oven to 350 degrees. Cut biscuits into four pieces and put into greased, baking dish. Pour sauce over biscuits and add any other options as preferred. Sprinkle grated cheese over top and bake for thirty minutes.

Italian Pot Roast

- 1–2 chuck roasts (2 pounds each)
- 2 onions sliced
- 4 potatoes
- 1 bag baby carrots
- 1 package zesty Italian salad dressing mix
- ½ jar pimento peppers
- 1 cup pepperocini peppers
- 2 cans beer

Cut roast into chunks and put into large pot or slow cooker. Add sliced onion, Italian salad dressing mix, pimento peppers, pepperocini peppers, and two cans of beer. Cook for six hours on low heat. Add carrots and chunked potatoes and cook for two more hours.

Marinade and Barbeque Sauce

- 1 cup brown sugar
- 1 cup of each:
    - Barbeque sauce
    - Ketchup
    - Liquid marinade (Mesquite or Hickory)
    - ½ bottle of beer
    - 1 tablespoon mustard
    - 1 tablespoon Italian seasoning
    - 1 tablespoon garlic
    - 1 tablespoon Barbeque spice or dry rub

(This recipe can also be prepared with wine instead of beer or one cup zesty Italian salad dressing instead of Italian seasoning.)

Combine all ingredients in a mixing bowl and stir until completely mixed. Taste and add any of the above in small increments to create the flavor you are looking for.

Pour over meat, chicken, pork, ribs, etc. and let set in fridge for at least one hour (can set overnight for optimum results).

Potatoes on the Grill

- 6–26 potatoes (depending on how hungry you are or how many people you need to feed)
- 1–2 large onions chopped
- 1 green pepper chopped
- 1 package fresh mushrooms
- 6–26 corn on the cobs
- 1–2 sticks of butter
- Smoked sausage
- Bratwursts
- Salt and pepper
- Italian seasoning

Lay out aluminum foil and spray with cooking spray. Slice potatoes and put in foil. Add onions, peppers, mushrooms, and any other veggies that you would want to add for flavor; salt and pepper to taste. Add a light dusting of Italian seasoning. Cut butter sticks into chunks and place on top of potatoes. Place corn cobs on top. Add Sausages or brats to top. Wrap all ingredients in foil to create a large cooking package. Place on grill with burners set on low for one hour to 1 ½ hour (depending on amount to be cooked).

Hamburgers and Steaks

Mix hamburger meat with any of the following:

- Dry Barbeque rub
- Dry onion soup mix
- Italian seasoning
- 2 tablespoons A1 sauce
- Garlic

Form meat into patties and place on grill. Cook on medium heat until done. Add sliced cheese if desired and place buns on top. Turn off burners and let set for about two minutes. Serve with favorite garnishes and French fries.

For best results, use the leanest possible hamburger

meat. This will cook up better with less shrinkage and less flame up due to excessive grease.

Steaks should be placed in marinade for at least two hours before cooking. Place on hot grill (burners on high) for about two minutes on each side (this will help sear in the juices). Turn burners down to medium and cook for remaining time until done to taste.

Barbeque Chicken

- Boneless/skinless chicken—amount to be determined by number of people to feed or how hungry you are.
- Marinade—see previous recipe.
- Pineapple slices

Marinade chicken for one to two hours. Cook on grill, turning regularly, and baste with extra marinade on each turn. Add pineapple slices to grill for about two minutes on each side. Place grilled pineapple on chicken for about two minutes prior to taking chicken off of grill

Pork chops, pork loin, or ham steaks can be cooked the same way

Baby Back Ribs

- 1–2 slabs of ribs
- Dry Barbeque rub
- Marinade (see previous recipe)

Place ribs in marinade and let set for at least two hours (overnight is best). With burners on low, place the ribs on the grill and dust lightly with dry rub; let cook for ten to fifteen minutes and turn. Brush with extra marinade and dust with dry rub. Turn and brush with marinade every ten to fifteen minutes for about 1 ½ hours until rib meat pulls easily from the bone.

Desserts

Not too long ago, I remember seeing a sign in a restaurant that said: "life is uncertain, eat dessert first." I had to chuckle, not because of the humor, but because of the truth of this statement. We too often save the best part until last, and in too many cases, never get to the best part. Why not start with the best part first?

With that in mind, I am going to refer you to the best for the recipes for desserts. I am not a baker of pies, cookies and cakes. I can buy a box of something and make it according to the noted recipe. However, there are people skilled in the art of baking that you will want to learn from. You will want to start spending time with your grandmother and Aunt Missy to learn more about baking. They can show you the ins and outs of how much a dash and pinch actually would be. They can teach you the fine art of making pie crust, cookies, cakes, and other delicacies from the oven.

Baking is an art which is acquired over years of practice. Unless you are particularly gifted in this area, you will need a mentor to help you along the way. Learning this art will pay back many dividends over the years ahead and save a lot of money over the purchase of pre-made, store bought items. I encourage you to take the time to learn the basics at least. Who knows, you could be the next Betty Crocker!